Anonymus

Yearbook 1898

Anonymus

Yearbook 1898

ISBN/EAN: 9783741178696

Manufactured in Europe, USA, Canada, Australia, Japa

Cover: Foto ©Paul-Georg Meister /pixelio.de

Manufactured and distributed by brebook publishing software (www.brebook.com)

Anonymus

Yearbook 1898

GENERAL VIEW.

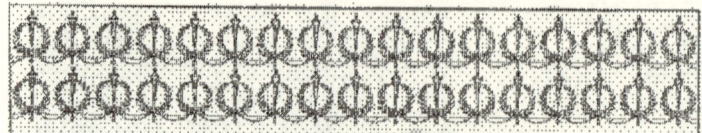

Published by the Junior Class
Rhode Island
College of Agriculture and Mechanic Arts.

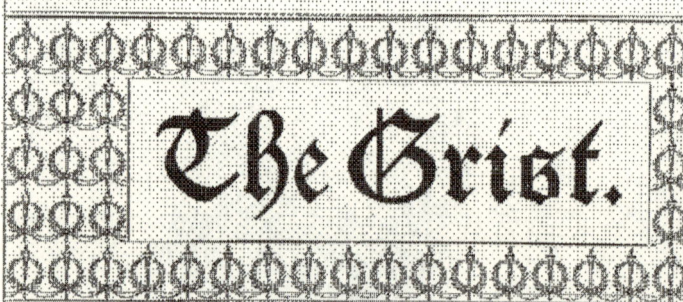

The Grist.

Second Volume.

Kingston, ... Rhode Island.

June, 1898.

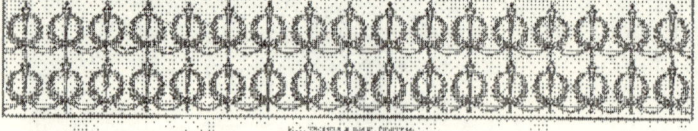

Contents.

Dedication.
Board of Editors.
Introduction.
College Calendar.
Board of Managers.
Faculty.
History of College During the Past Year.
The Prof.'s Hunt for Grounds.
Classes.
'Neath the Hood.
A Glorious Achievement.
Sketches—Courses of Study.
Brave Sophomores.
Lippitt Hall.
In Memoriam.
General Calendar.
Applied Quotations.
Nonsense.
Manuscripts for Sale.
Military Companies.
Clubs.
Associations.
Advertisements.

TO

Captain W. W. Wotherspoon,

WE,

WHO APPRECIATE HIS KINDLY INTEREST AND HELP,

DEDICATE

THIS VOLUME.

Board of Editors.

Editor-in-Chief.

E. PAYNE.

Assistant Editors.

HARRY KNOWLES.   SALLY R. THOMPSON.

BLYDON E. KENYON.

Business Manager and Secretary.

ALFRED W. BOSWORTH.

Introduction.

DEAR READER:
Since we were appointed by our class to prepare "The Grist" of '99, we have passed through fearful trials and tribulations. Oh! the sleepless nights, and the dreams haunted by original conundrums and old jokes. If our hair is not gray we are indeed thankful. Our staff is a model one, each member wishing to be boss and not wanting to work, so that whenever we met for business there was more scrapping than anything else. After a while, however, we realized that, although we were all to be bosses, we should each have to do his share of work; so we threw all our energies into the task of sorting and putting into some sort of order the chaos of literary productions with which we had been deluged. Alas! it was a hopeless task; for after weeks of superhuman effort we gave way beneath the strain. Only two more days

were left in which to have the copy ready for the printer. "The Grist" must be published, so we selected at random from the great pile of MS. the rubbish which you will find in the following pages. If, dear reader, there should be anything in them to hurt your feelings, we would advise you to seek out the writer and get satisfaction; but do not ask us to help you, for our task is done, and we are tired.

College Calendar.

1898.
Winter Term.

January 3, 1 P. M.,	Term begins.
January 27,	Day of Prayer for Colleges.
February 22,	Washington's Birthday.
March 25,	Term ends.

Spring Term.

April 4,	Term begins.
————	Arbor Day.
May 30,	Memorial Day.
June 6,	Senior Examinations begin.
June 12,	Baccalaureate Sunday.
June 14,	Commencement.
June 18, 10 A. M.,	Entrance Examinations.

Fall Term.

September 1, 2, 10 A. M.,	Entrance Examinations.
September 19, 20, 10 A. M.,	Examination of Conditioned Students.
September 19, 20, 10 A. M.,	Entrance Examinations.
September 21, 1 P. M.,	Term begins.
————	Thanksgiving Day.
December 22,	Term ends.

1899.
Winter Term.

January 2,	Examination of Conditioned Students.
January 3, 1 P. M.,	Term begins.
March 24,	Term ends.

Spring Term.

April 3,	Examination of Conditioned Students.
April 4, 1 P. M.,	Term begins.
June 11,	Baccalaureate Sunday.
June 13,	Term ends.

Board of Managers.

Corporation.

Hon. Melville Bull,	*Newport County.*
Hon. H. C. Coggeshall,	*Bristol County.*
Hon. Jesse V. B. Watson,	*Washington County.*
Hon. Henry L. Greene,	*Kent County.*
Hon. Gardiner C. Sims,	*Providence County.*

Officers of Corporation.

Hon. C. H. Coggeshall, *President,*	P. O., Bristol, R. I.
Hon. Henry L. Greene, *Vice-President,*	P. O., Riverpoint, R. I.
Hon. Gardiner C. Sims, *Clerk,*	P. O., Providence, R. I.
Hon. Melville Bull, *Treasurer,*	P. O., Newport, R. I.

Faculty.

JOHN HOSEA WASHBURN, Ph. D.,
PRESIDENT.
Professor of Agricultural Chemistry.

HOMER JAY WHEELER, Ph. D.,
Professor of Geology.

ANNE LUCY BOSWORTH, B. S.,
Professor of Mathematics.

E. JOSEPHINE WATSON, A. M.,
Professor of Languages.

WILLIAM ELISHA DRAKE, B. S.,
Professor of Mechanical Engineering.

OLIVER CHASE WIGGIN, M. D.,
Professor of Comparative Anatomy and Physiology.

WILLIAM WALLACE WOTHERSPOON,
Captain, 12th Infantry, U. S. A.,
Professor of Military Science and Tactics.

HARRIET LATHROP MERROW, A. M.,
Professor of Botany.

ARTHUR AMBER BRIGHAM, Ph. D.,
Professor of Agriculture.

GEORGE WILTON FIELD, Ph. D.,
Professor of Zoölogy.

FRED WALLACE CARD, M. S.,
Professor of Horticulture.

JAMES DE LOSS TOWAR, B. S.,
Assistant Professor of Agriculture and in Charge of Civil Engineering

JOHN EMERY BUCHER, A. C., Ph. D.,
Professor of Chemistry.

ARTHUR CURTIS SCOTT, B. S.,
Instructor in Physics.

MABEL DE WITT ELDRED, B. S.,
Instructor in Drawing.

MARY WATKINSON ROCKWELL, B. S.,
Instructor in Languages.

LUCY HARRIET PUTMAN,
Instructor in Expression.

THOMAS CARROLL RODMAN,
Instructor in Woodwork.

HELEN ELIZABETH BROOKS,
Instructor in Stenography and Typewriting.

CHARLES SHERMAN CLARKE, B. S.,
Assistant in Mechanics.

JOHN FRANKLIN KNOWLES, B. S.,
Assistant in Woodwork.

HOWLAND BURDICK, B. S.,
Assistant in Agriculture.

CHARLES FRANKLIN KENYON, B. S.,
Assistant in Chemistry.

LOUIS HERBERT MARSLAND, B. S.,
Assistant in Mathematics.

GEORGE BURLEIGH KNIGHT,
Instructor in Ironwork.

NATHANIEL HELME.

History of College during the Past Year.

THE improvements at the college during the past year have exceeded in number and importance those in any one preceding year.

The buildings have received names in honor of the governors who were in office at the time the appropriations for building were made. The dormitory is called Davis Hall; the experiment station building, Taft Laboratory; the mechanical building, Ladd Laboratory; and the new building, which has been completed during the past year, Lippitt Hall. This last is a noble looking structure, built of granite from the college quarry. Over the entrance is the State seal carved in granite. There are but three floors; the first containing the physical laboratory, the electrical laboratory, and the engine room, in which is kept the printing press for doing the college printing. On the second floor are two recitation rooms, a lecture room, the young ladies' study room, and the library, which is under the supervision of a regular librarian. The third floor is a spacious drill hall. It is one of the finest halls in this part of the country, being one hundred and thirty-eight feet long, and having a seating capacity of one thousand. The acquisition of this building not only increases the facilities for work, but also makes it possible to develop social life at the college.

The barracks and carpenter's shop have been moved east of Lippitt Hall, and the interior of the former has been converted into a chemical laboratory and lecture room. This laboratory is much larger, and, because of its excellent hoods, better than the one formerly used in Taft Laboratory. These buildings have been moved for the purpose of clearing the campus.

The government has built half a mile of sample road around the campus, which greatly facilitates travel, as the chief characteristic of Kingston soil is mud.

There were so many applications for admission to Watson House that the two attic rooms on the third floor were furnished; but even these additions proved insufficient for the demand. During the winter the M. E. M. G. F. G. Club connected with Watson House gave a very successful entertainment, the proceeds of which were used for the improvement of the reception room.

One destructive feature entered with all this prosperity, and that was a slight damage done to the botanical laboratory by fire. The professor of botany was the most seriously affected by the loss of her herbarium.

The new members of the faculty are Miss Rockwell, who succeeded Miss Peckham; Miss Eldred, who succeeded Miss Helme; Dr. Bucher, professor of chemistry; C. F. Kenyon, assistant chemist; and L. H. Marsland, assistant in mathematics.

Those who have watched the growth of the institution fully appreciate these improvements, and we hope the coming volumes of "The Grist" will be able to relate further and greater successes than have yet been accomplished.

The Professor's Hunt for Grounds.

A Prof. one day a-hunting went
   Ground circuits new to find.
He on this quest was so intent
   Nought else could fill his mind.

And when a shaky joint was found
   In Johnny Wilby's room,
He spread the news for miles around—
   His face with joy did bloom.

Through the tin cup he thought he could
   A nice short circuit get,
And that it came right through the wood,
   He willing was to bet.

He to the engine room did go,
   All joints with tape he wrapped;
He hunted all day, high and low,
   To see if wires were tapped.

That circuit through the old tin cup
   A mystery will remain,
Unless the secret's given up
   By naughty Mr. Payne.

Of currents from a magneto
   We've heard, when turned by hand;
But how a shock through wood could go
   We'll never understand.

WATSON HOUSE.

The Classes.

"1901."

CLASS COLORS: Crimson and White.

WE have now nearly completed three terms of college life, and it is with pride that we submit to the public the record of our events.

On the 21st of September, 1897, we entered the Rhode Island College. We were not long in making acquaintances among the upper classmen, and we found them to be a genial set of young people; although at first they sometimes sent us to the wrong places, or told us "Bear Stories." During the first few weeks our efforts to appear decorous must have caused much amusement among the other classes, but that is no more.

When we selected our class pins, some of the members wished to have them of a different design from that used at present; but, when the other classes and the faculty asked us to keep the old design, we agreed not to make any change.

In October the Juniors gave a reception to our class, at which we made many new acquaintances, and received our first impressions of college society.

For the most part the Sophomores have refrained from troubling the Freshman; a few of them did, however, try to give us some "Cold Baths," but they retired with more speed than grace.

The Class had no football team of its own, during the season of '97, but it showed its ability in combining with the Sophomores, and winning each of the several games played. We also had several members on the "varsity" eleven, which is in itself a very great honor, and one of which few classes can boast. Early in the spring we formed a base-ball team, which has amply upheld the honor of its class.

Of course we have our "curios," as has every class; we are proud to have "Sousa" in our midst, also several other musicians of note. Our "mascot" always brings good luck; he was prominent on each of the above-mentioned "elevens," which to any well informed person explains itself. His favorite pastime is dancing the Schottische.

Well! we are only Freshmen now, but soon we "cross the awful chasm" and become Sophomores. Then let the Freshmen beware for we prophesy trouble; and now we bid you good-bye, until we meet you again in the next "Grist."

C. G. A.

Freshman Class.

CLASS YELL: Here we Come! Here we Come!
The Noble Class of 1901!

Officers.

L. G. K. CLARNER, JR., PRESIDENT.
W. S. MOFFITT, VICE-PRESIDENT.
L. J. REUTER, SECRETARY.
D. CAMPBELL, TREASURER.

MISS M. W. ROCKWELL, *Honorary Member.*

Members.

CARLTON G. ANDREWS	*Potter Hill.*
EDWIN T. ARNOLD	*Woonsocket.*
NELLIE A. BRIGGS	*Shannock.*
CHARLES S. BURGESS	*Providence.*
ISABEL N. CLARK	*Usquepaug.*
EDNA E. DAWLEY	*Kenyon.*
WILLIAM J. DAWLEY	*Kenyon.*
ARTHUR A. DENICO	*Narragansett Pier.*
ERNEST GRAHAM	*Wakefield.*
ROBERT E. GRINNELL	*Middletown.*
CHARLES H. S. HARROWER	*Peace Dale.*
FANNY L. HOPKINS	*Plainfield, Conn.*
HENRY O. HOPKINS	*Plainfield, Conn.*
GARABAD KREKORIAN	*Harpoot, Turkey.*
EARLE A. LANDERS	*Newport.*
CHARLES A. LECLAIR	*Bristol.*
DUDLEY NEWTON, JR.	*Newport.*
SARAH W. D. PALMER	*Wakefield.*
THOMAS C. RILEY	*Lafayette.*
ARTHUR A. SHERMAN	*Portsmouth.*
ANNA B. SHERMAN	*Kingston.*
ELIZABETH A. SHERMAN	*West Kingston.*
HOWARD D. SMITH	*North Scituate.*
FANNY E. STILLMAN	*Kenyon.*
EMILY P. WELLS	*Kingston.*
CHARLES W. WILCOX	*Kingston.*

1900.

CLASS COLORS: White and Gold.

CLASS YELL: Whoop-la-ra! Whoop-la-ree!

Walk up! Chalk up! Upidee!

1900! Yes-sir-ree!

WHEN we took leave of you a year ago, we promised to "see you later;" and as we are men of our word, "*nous voici*." (Please observe that we have studied French since we saw you last.)

We are sorry to have lost some of our members, but, as we have gained an equal number, we still have a membership of thirty.

We cannot deny that there are some very strange things about this class of 1900. One notable fact is that we always "Fry" our game. The class has certainly been growing too "Cross" of late, and it is not so "Jollie" as formerly, yet it has a large "Soul(e)." One of our number is called Greene, but we also have a Brightman who looks after our understanding. Another fellow has been a Wheeler all his life, yet his achievements in mathematics are even more brilliant than his cycling record. One of our young ladies is very fond of taking shocks, and of catching Arachnida, ophidia, Lepidoptera, bacertilia, shy chophiladee, Lamellibranchiata, and other such creatures, but these things never seem to "Hurter." The proposition in one of the early Sophomore class meetings to receive a Sp(h)inx among our number was at first rather startling, but we concluded that we could "Tucker" in.

Some members of the class have been electing expression, and when a particularly large blot alights on a particularly fine mechanical drawing there is conclusive evidence that they have not studied in vain.

We had no chance to immortalize ourselves by building a drill shed, and we have been so unfortunate as to lose our Carpenter, but we think we shall yet be able to demonstrate that the class of '99 is not the only one gifted with architectural abilities.

The evening of March eleventh is one we shall long remember. At that time Miss Putnam received her classmates at Watson House. The hours passed merrily, and as we left the air rang with cheers for our honorary member.

We hold no ill will against the Freshmen for refusing us an opportunity to beat them at foot-ball. We welcome them to the place which, in the course of college events, we must soon vacate; with all the privileges and appurtenances thereto belonging, not excepting the mysteries of Trig and Chemistry, while we "Steere" our way as "Wells" we may toward the joys and perplexities of Junior life.

It is with sincere regret that we say good-bye to the class of '98; yet it is a pleasure to acknowledge the courtesy and kindness they have always shown us, and to give them our heartiest good wishes as they go out from us and from their Alma Mater.

Sophomore Class.

Officers.

A. E. MUNRO, PRESIDENT.
MISS S. L. JAMES, VICE PRESIDENT.
MISS E. M. PARKHURST, SECRETARY.
A. PEARSON, TREASURER.

Honorary Member.

MISS LUCY HARRIET PUTNAM . . . . Newton, Mass.

Members.

WILLIAM BALLOU ARNOLD	Woonsocket.
GLEN ISAAC BRIGGS	Woonsocket.
HENRY MASON BRIGHTMAN	White Rock.
LATHAM CLARKE	West Kingston.
CHARLES CLARK CROSS	Narragansett Pier.
MORTON ROBINSON CROSS	Wakefield.
JOHN RALEIGH ELDRED	Kingston.
JOHN JAMES FRY	East Greenwich.
EDITH GODDARD	Brockton, Mass.
PRESCOTT MORRILL GREENE	Peace Dale.
FLORENCE DUDLEY HUNTER	Somerville, Mass.
RUTH HORTENSE JAMES	Kenyon.
SARAH LILA JAMES	Kenyon.
AMOS LANGWORTHY KENYON	Wood River Junction.
LEROY WESTON KNOWLES	Point Judith.
ELISHA FREDERIC LAMPHERE	Peace Dale.
ARTHUR EARLE MUNRO	Quonochontaug.
ABBIE FIDELIA NORTHUP	Wickford.
ELIZABETH MAY PARKHURST	Wickford.
ALFRED PEARSON, JR.	Newburyport, Mass.
ROBERT JOSEPH SHERMAN	Usquepaug.
GEORGE CANNING SOULE	Wickford.
RALPH NELSON SOULE	Wickford.
MYRA BERTINE SPINK	Wickford.
ANTHONY ENOCH STEERE	Chepachet.
BERTHA DOUGLAS TUCKER	Swansea Centre, Mass.
HERBERT COMSTOCK WELLS	Kingston.
LEVI EUGENE WIGHTMAN	South Scituate.
JOSEPH ROBERT WILSON	Allenton.
CHARLES NOYES WHEELER	Shannock.

Junior Class.

CLASS COLORS: Blue and Pink.

Miss Peckham, our former instructor in English, and an honorary member of our class, left at the close of last year to attend the Leland Stanford University, in California. We regret her departure, and her presence among us has been greatly missed.

Miss Merrow, professor of botany, very kindly consented to become an honorary member of our class. Her help and friendship have been a great pleasure to us, and are thoroughly appreciated by all.

Alfred Willson Bosworth is a man of muscle. His highest ambition is to become a captain and wear a sword. How he used to envy that inimitable strut that Gossie had when he was a captain! He is very susceptible to the charms of the fair ones of our number, and it has been reported that he may often be seen on Sunday afternoons and evenings in the vicinity of  Watson House, and not always alone. He had the honor to succeed Bill Gump as physical laboratory assistant. We would advise him to take a lesson from Gump's fall from grace, and not know too much of practical ELECTRICITY, or the history may be repeated.

CLIFFORD BREWSTER MORRISON. Tread softly, bow thy head in lowly reverence; humble thyself before this mighty intellect which has appeared in our midst, whose equal never crossed the threshold of the R. I. C. Never was there brain that held so much. He is an authority on bacteria. Of chemistry he knows everything. In biology he can give the professor points. When, in the botanical laboratory, he explains the chemical reactions going on in the cells of plants, we are awed into wondering admiration, and the professor meekly subsides into silent recognition of a superior mind.

MERRILL A. LADD. How he loves to lord it in the boarding hall. As he struts around the tables like a little bantam rooster, his expression proclaims the fact that he is monarch of all he surveys. His frown of disgust, when some poor, hungry student has the audacity to ask for more, is indescribable. He is a very bright lad in matters pertaining to electricity, and we have been  told that without his help the storage battery would never have been in the almost useless condition in which it now is.

WILLIAM F. OWEN. "Whistle and she'll come to you my lad." He can cut ice with any girl in the place, but, being a true sport, he does not care for game which comes too easily to his net, so he goes hunting in Peacedale, where the girls are more shy. He is captain of the ball team, and is noted for the clean game he plays at football.

E. PAYNE, ye ancient one, called papa by some of the younger members of the class, who, however, do not show him the respect which such a name should command. He is a living example of the demoralizing effect of environment, for he came here a staid old man; but the surrounding influence has so affected him that, although he has never been caught, we believe that he is up to more boyish devilment than any of the youngsters ever thought of. Ask him  who fastened the smoking-room door and waited at the second story with a pail of water, ready to soak the smokers as they escaped by the window. Who sent the shock through the OLD TIN CUP.

 SALLY RODMAN THOMPSON has a great fondness for mathematics and for bossing the show. You may see her any morning scurrying off to the class in mathematics—the lower branches—as though she wanted to get there before she forgot her lesson. One day in class the following axiom was formulated: "It's so, if it isn't so, if Sally says so."

BLYDON E. KENYON is a good, honest member of the class. He minds his own business, and has not made himself conspicuous by the development of any special idiosyncracies. He is a great favorite with all the girls of the class.

JOHN STUART CUMMINGS loves study and drill above all other good things. He is especially stuck on German, and would rather study that than have a good dinner. Ask him, if you don't believe us.

HENRY F. W. ARNOLD is a young man with a taste for "Degeneration." A true morbid deviation from an original type. His lingering refrain, "Am I an accidental concatenation of parts?" Perhaps so, my boy; but then, true blood always tells.

Point Judith has brought forth many illustrious sons, but none more so than HARRY KNOWLES. He began his college work at the age of fifteen, disturbing our morning slumbers by ringing the bell at 6:30 every morning, studying biology and agriculture. He aspires to become a Ph. D., and will get his degree, even if he has to buy one in Germany. In *affairs du cœur* he is considered by many to be an adept, but we know of one vulnerable spot in his heart.

MILDRED WAYNE HARVEY is a very ambitious girl, and had a very high standing in her class until a measly time came along. From this she has not yet wholly recovered, but hopes to, soon. She is an active worker in some of the societies, and generally holds some office, and acts often as a delegate. She has been secretary of the class for three years, and will probably keep that office till we graduate.

ROBERT S. REYNOLDS came here from Wickford. He is an excellent waiter, when he is not asleep, and is a prominent member of the athletic association. He says that when he is president of a college he will let the students have every day off for athletic sports.

GEORGE A. SHERMAN. Some persons think that George A. Sherman has missed his calling in becoming a mechanical student, and that he ought to have stuck to farming. He has been carrying on some original research in mechanics, and expects to solve the problem of perpetual motion soon. Although this young gentleman comes from the country, he can give some of the city boys a few points in most subjects.

WALTER C. PHILLIPS is president of the class of '99. He is a straight mechanical student, and gets much enjoyment out of machine-shop work. 'Tis said that the belt is constantly slipping off the pulley of his lathe, but instead of losing patience with it, he is contented to sit down and take it easy until the instructor comes along and replaces it for him. His great ambition is to take life easy.

CARROLL KNOWLES is the only Kingston man in the class. He is a great student of languages, and has especially distinguished himself in French and German. As a mathematician no one in the class can beat him. At class meetings he supports every motion that is made, and was never known to take the negative side.

MINNIE E. RICE is from Wickford, and is taking the straight scientific course. She expects to become a schoolmarm, so, as a preparation for her future work, she is taking agricultural chemistry. Her executive ability is great, as was shown by the way she carried out her duties as a member of the Arbor Day committee.

GERTRUDE S. FISON comes daily from Peacedale. She takes all the studies of the Junior scientifics, with the exception of English; which, however, she would have taken, had not the professor of that branch told her that she was not advanced enough in years to take such an advanced study. At tackling social problems she is an adept, for she planned and managed our reception to the Freshmen with great skill.

'98.

CLASS COLORS : Blue and White.
**CLASS YELL : Rah ! rah ! rah ! Never late,
We're the Class of '98 ! Rah !**

OUR most promising student of evolution has departed to unknown regions in search of hidden mysteries, so the history of the Senior class, which is necessarily of an evolutionary character, cannot be presented in that precise and logical order which marks the productions of such individuals.

The progress of the class during the past year has been most marked, but no less distinct are the changes wrought in the individuals. Indeed, I believe that the personality of the various members stands out more prominently before the outside observer than does the advancement of the class collectively. It is perhaps well that this is so; for when the time comes for united effort, as it will in the near future, the class of '98 will not be found wanting.

We have perhaps seen more changes at the college than has any other class, for, when such events as fires and restorations could no longer claim our attention, we have been busy trying some new venture, which has generally been successful, and has often proved a precedent to other classes.

We all supposed astrology was something of past ages, never more to return; so nothing could create greater astonishment, no, not even the report that the Spanish navy commanded by Alphonso XX. was upon Lake Laurel, than did the notice read in chapel stating that all the students were assigned to certain members of the faculty, who would be their guiding star to advise, foretell, and rule their destinies. Those who do not understand the facts of the case declare that at present we are surrounded by a mantle of life and one of death. They say that the mantle of life is bright and unmistakable, for it embodies, among other things, a high hope for the future. This is quite true, but when questioned about the mantle of death they try to seek a connection between it and the modern astrology, saying that as we have several doctors as guiding stars, and that one month of doctor's care will kill a sick man and two a well one, there is really very little hope for us. This is wholly untrue, for they have confounded the new astrology with the old, and perhaps the physicians of our modern times with the ancients, or, what is more likely, with our modern quacks.

Our honorary member, Miss Bosworth, we regret to say, will not be able to be with us at commencement, for she soon sails over the ocean. *Bon voyage*, we shall not forget. At an evening gathering in her house she presented the class with an ivy, which will be planted on class day, when our poet, orator, and speakers will shed forth the glory of their eloquence and genius; but this will be near commencement, the day to which we now look forward.

Senior Class.

Officers.

H. A. CONGDON, PRESIDENT.
G. T. ROSE, VICE-PRESIDENT.
W. C. CLARKE, SECRETARY.
MISS WILSON, TREASURER.

Executive Committee.

J. P. CASE.   W. F. HARLEY.   W. C. CLARKE.

Honorary Member.

MISS ANNIE L. BOSWORTH   *Kingston.*

Members.

SARAH ESTELLE ARNOLD	*Wakefield.*
GEORGE WASHINGTON BARBER	*Shannock.*
EDNA MARIA CARGILL	*Abbott Run.*
JOHN P. CASE	*Gould.*
WILLIAM CASE CLARKE	*Wakefield.*
HENRY AUGUSTUS CONGDON	*Kingston.*
MARTHA REBECCA FLAGG	*Kingston.*
WILLIAM FERGUSON HARLEY	*Pawtucket.*
GEORGE TUCKER ROSE	*Kingston.*
HARRIETTE FLORENCE TURNER	*Ontario Centre, N. Y.*
GRACE ELLEN WILSON	*Allenton.*

'Neath The Hood.

Once upon a day so dreary, while we pondered, bright and cheery,
　Each one o'er a new and curious volume of chemical lore—
While we listened, no, not napping, suddenly there came a tapping
　As of some one lightly walking, walking to the class-room door.
"'Tis the doctor," some one muttered, "walking to the class-room
　　door "—
　This it was that stopped the roar.

Ah, distinctly we remember it was in the glad September,
　When the doctor, mild and tender, book in hand before us stood.
" Now this book will be quite ample, each before you has a sample,
　But before we further trample, let me now suggest some food
For your future good and guidance, when you work beneath the
　　hood,
　'Neath the better, larger hood."

" First of all the mysteries solving, and the work on you devolving
　Is for you to group correctly all the metals as you should,
In solutions that I give you—the reagents that are needed
　HCl by H_2S succeeded, since the odor is not good.
And in fact I should advise you, if the odor is not good,
　Always work beneath the hood."

This was but an introduction to the hood with its seduction—
  Little did the mild professor, as he spake in kindly mood,
Think of all the fascination and the varied conversation,
  That the students with elation carried on across the hood
Oh, the cookies that were eaten by the few who understood—
  As they waited 'neath the hood.

But the course is now completed, and although we're not conceited,
  Still we feel somewhat elated that our work has been so good.
Thinking not of things we've broken, nor of tests which have
    bespoken
  Much " magruffen," wretched token, we would linger if we could;
But the thought is thrust upon us nevermore beneath the hood,
  'Neath the better, larger hood.

A Glorious Achievement.

THE saddest event in the history of our college, or any other institution, occurred Thursday afternoon, May 19, 1898, on the college athletic field. After vanquishing their brethren of 1900 in the ball game, the Freshmen never stopped till they achieved the right to carry canes forever upon the college grounds. It was a famous victory, marked by wonderful and glorious deeds, unparalleled in any conflict recorded in history.

That awful struggle would surely have continued till now if it had not been for some of our respected alumni, who, out of pity for 1900, broke up the conflict before serious injuries occurred.

The struggle for the cane was brought about in this manner: Considerable feeling having been aroused by the inglorious defeat sustained by the Sophomores, one of their number, he of "Regal Shoe" fame, over-zealous in his regard for a Sophomore victory, conceived the idea of forcing the Freshmen to give up the right of carrying canes. His eye fell upon a diminutive individual from Phenix, who was bravely parading about with one of the coveted sticks. Action immediately began, and, in a second, Mother Earth was covered with a swaying, battling mass of excited humanity. Legs and arms, but no heads nor bodies, shins were scraped, and heads were banged, the solar plexus especially receiving a full share of bruises; whilst from the pile came yells and invocations to Mars and all the gods of war. Here and there about the pile little groups were struggling; blood soon showed itself, and the whole country became tinged with a red light.

The Sophomores were getting worsted; and the charitable-minded alumni, after much hard labor, managed to separate the combatants and to restore peace. The college awarded the cane to the Freshies, and we all hope they'll stand by their colors as they did that May afternoon. But there'll be no need of such efforts, for the whole world knows what happened after supper, on the college road, for the Sophomores are humilated and crushed beyond recovery. This is the second time that 1900 has bitten the dust, for good old '99 beat them with a vengeance. We showed them up to the world then, and thought, perhaps, they'd take heed and brace up; but '01 showed they couldn't or wouldn't, so we have lost all faith in them. But there is some good blood in the class, and if they take advantage of it they may come out all right.

Sketches of Courses of Study.

Agriculture.

IN opening the college catalogue and looking through the classes, one would conclude that but a small portion of the students are farmers' sons. But in the Junior class there are actually as many as two taking the Agricultural course. Graduates of this school do not carry out the design of the course, but rather spend their energies as expressed in the words of Jethro Tull. "They think it more eligible to study the art of plowing the sea with ships than of tilling the land with plows; and regard it beneath men of learning to employ their learned labours in the invention of new instruments for increasing of bread."

As an inducement to lead a rural life a course in "Farm Management" is required in the first term of the Freshman year, which consists of picturing to the student the profit derived from the use of improved farm implements; also in furnishing the proper training for the selection of a location when they come to enjoy the pleasures of running a farm, while burdening them with definitions such as "A wall is a fence, but a fence is not necessarily a wall," and many other agricultural terms. Besides all these benefits, there is also that of mental training derived in trying to decipher one's own hieroglyphics after one has hurriedly taken notes on a lecture.

Then, passing on, we arrive at the study of "Farm Accounts," upon which we spent many happy hours pondering over account books, or devising some scheme by which to make the accounts balance, and thereby securing a good big "A."

Next comes what we thought to be the useless "Drainage," in which we were obliged to tax our brain to determine the depth a ditch should be dug in order to have the necessary fall, at the same time keeping the tile in a straight line; but now, on looking back, all agree it should have been placed first, for one, waking up at night and finding himself confronted with three or four pails of H_2O, commences to think of tile and its uses.

With the commencement of the Soph year comes the critical moment for the decision whether or no to take the Aggie course, and for the benefit of the class of '99 the professor of agriculture offered to pay the admission to the county fair of all those who would take the agricultural course. This was too great a temptation for two of us to resist.

The first study we took up was that of "Breeds of Live Stock." Many were the hours we passed in tracing out the pedigrees of different animals.

At the same time we studied the subject of "Farm Crops," in which we learned what varieties of crops could be grown together, also their chief characteristics. It was while studying this subject that we learned an astonishing fact, one morning, when the Prof. asked how to plant peas. This is the answer he received: "In hills, four feet apart each way." Perhaps that student had in mind the ideal method of intertillage of which we have heard so much.

Nevertheless, there is one study in the agricultural course from which some pleasure is derived, and that is civil engineering. For, when out with the transit surveying some piece of land, or perhaps laying out a road, we can spot a pretty girl in the distance by simply focusing the telescope on her, and none is any the wiser. On such days we are the envy of the Mechanics, who have by this time realized that machine shop work is not as pleasant as they at first thought it to be.

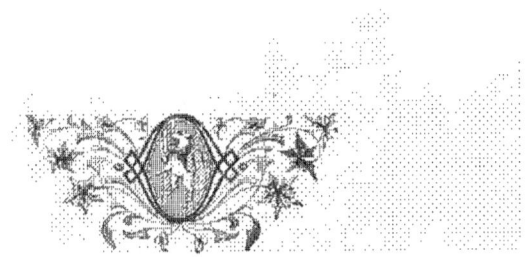

Mechanical Course.

All through the first year here at Kingston every student has a problem to solve. It is a question which we often hear asked, but very seldom answered: "Which course are you going to take?" It is not for us to philosophize, so we cannot say why most of our young men take the mechanical course. Possibly it is because they have an antipathy for the rake and hoe, or it may be they believe that their mind contains the latent genius of a Fulton or a Watts; however, be that as it may, the fact remains the same.

The first distinctly mechanical study of the course is wood-turning. Many curious adventures occur here. One day a young man was manipulating a piece of soft wood. His fastenings not being the most secure, the stick was liberated, and, whirling through the air, hit him squarely over the eye. It is safe to wager that "Prof. Holder" never saw more stars in the heavens on a frosty November night than our young man saw in his narrow horizon for a few seconds.

But our young men have done something more than meet with these unfortunate adventures. They have supplied the gymnasium with Indian clubs of their own production. We hope that when our gymnasium shall be better equipped that these clubs will be saved as a relic of a former generation or some other equally good cause.

But we pass on to the forging of iron, which is our next occupation. Such an admirable forge-shop as we have. There is only one fault: at certain times, particularly when the afternoon's work is beginning, the atmosphere becomes thick with smoke, resembling an aggravated London fog. You cannot see your next neighbor, but occasionally can catch a glance of red hot iron. But that smoke! Well, it is right there, and stays until one feels like saying "How long, O Lord, how long."

But one feature of forging is that it does not last forever, although difficulties thicken all the time. And when you are perched up on a ladder in the top of the machine-shop, sweltering with heat, and using vain phrases endeavoring to replace a refractory belt on the pulleys, you can almost wish yourself back in the thick atmosphere of the forge-shop. But, about the belt, there is a most excellent way of replacing one. First get your ladder placed right (this is essential), then ascend upon it, get to your belt, fumble round five minutes, then go and tell the instructor that you cannot replace it. Luckily he can do it, so you are all right again. Napoleon said: "The tools belong to those who can use them," and so that is one way of replacing a belt.

All this goes to prove that the way of the would-be mechanic is not always strewn with roses; and if you are going to be a mechanic you must take the bad along with the good, the bitter with the sweet.

Chemistry.

Our course in chemistry is like the beautiful, "a joy forever." We shall always think of our chem. lab. days as happy ones. Now it is very sad, but there are a few individuals in college who will very heartily refute these statements. Take as an example Mr. Second Floor Senior, first door to the left. Imagine, if you will, the consternation and rage of that youth when he reads these lines. There will be weeping, wailing, and gnashing of teeth in more than one happy home.

Nevertheless, we, the lovers, the worshipers at the shrine of chemistry, and *à bas* with those who oppose. For our theoretical course we refer you to pages 23, 42, 43, 67, 67, 71, in the college catalogue of '97. The reader will please note that we lead the list of studies and courses. We are at the top, have always been there, and always will.

Our faculty consists of President Washburn, Dr. Bucher, and of course we will not forget Prof. Charles F. Kenyon, lab. assistant and general "get-there-or-die man." In passing, Kenyon has an office on the left side of the chem. lab., next to the centre hood. Visitors admitted once in a great while.

We consider ourselves fortunate, the favored ones, as we always are, in having with us such an instructor as Dr. Bucher. If it were pardonable to eulogize, we would with a will. Dr. Bucher has our respect and confidence.

We have a well-equipped laboratory, although the roof does leak. Everything considered, the college has done well by us, but we could still utilize many things. We are not jealous of the Physics crowd, even if they do own Lippitt Hall.

In closing let us say once more "We are the people," free sulphuric-acid soda water forever, and long life to the Chemical course!!

Biology.

"Hullo, there! No. 312,896. What, you back here!" said the clerk in the packing room of the B—— and L—— microscope manufactories.

"Take me out at once," replied a weak voice all smothered in cotton, "and carry me to the repair shop, for I've no time to lose."

"So they used you roughly; did they, old fellow? Come now, sit on the shelf and tell me what you saw and where you have been, while I see what is the matter."

"Well," began the microscope in the same weak voice, "when you packed me to be sent, and took me down to the station, someone stuck a big tag on me, and I never knew what it said. After I had traveled a great distance I was thrown off at Kingston, R. I., and struck wrong side up on the platform. Someone who was there paid the express bill, and grumbled because it was so large; while I was glad when he gave me to a big boy with a rough and ready voice, and I was carried off up a hill. I liked that boy, and I knew he was getting ten cents an hour, because he worked so carefully."

"The next morning I was unwrapped by a lady who took me out of my box. Then I found myself in a small, cheap, wooden building of one room. Several students were there at the time. She said I was the brightest of them all, and soon a boy was directed to come and take me. It is to him that I owe my first peep at the outside world. He was a green fellow, grabbed me by my nose piece, nearly breaking it off, and set me down on his desk with a thud. He then scraped some green stuff from a piece of bark, mounted it, and turned on the highest power, only to have it ordered away by the professor in charge.

"'Protococus is a unicellular plant,' the instructor was saying; 'but, Oh my! Just look for yourself and see these little green masses floating around. Only to think that these are plants! There is one dividing into two—no, it is two; but listen, the process of reproduction is by cell division. Yes, now you have it all, the Ontogeny or life history.'"

"'On what side of the tree does this plant grow?' the professor asked, and the same naughty boy whispered 'on the outside.' Upon taking another peep his eyes became tired, and I was given to a girl who spilled HCl. upon my objective the first thing; this had to be wiped off by a particular kind of paper. She then looked at some yeast plants. These are nearly colorless bodies, and often I saw one with a large bud on it which eventually became another plant."

"One night I began to grow very warm and felt uneasy, when I heard someone cry 'Fire! Fire!' I knew positively that it was the botanical laboratory, and sure enough it was. The hose-cart was soon brought by the Sophomores, and a stream of water flooded the room. I was taken to a large stone building for safety. Someone put me under a shelf, and nobody knew where I was until one day a young man came in to study bacteriology. I was hauled over the coals in fine style, and soon had to view the much dreaded microbes. He was very careless and sloppy, never dreaming they might injure me, but always disinfecting his knife with which he transferred them. Even this excitement grew monotonous, and when the histology class was formed the instructor said: 'Well, my friend, you do look worn out, you surely need a rest.' So here I am. What! all ready to go back? Now, box me up, and I will go over my journey again."

Scientific.

This course is offered to those students who desire a general education. It is not by any means the most difficult course offered, as some of the subjects given might lead one to think. It embraces many subjects, and it sometimes happens that several students of the same year have nothing in common.

The paths of this course which are most frequently trodden, are, botany, physics, chemistry, and general biology; of which physics seems to be the most thorny. The present Senior class seemed to have a special affection for chemistry in their junior year; indeed, in the winter term they were so constantly in the chemical laboratory that it was impossible to enter that building at any time of the day without meeting some of them. We think this example shows how the chemistry has been appreciated by former students.

It has been said that the scientific course is the one to take if a student wishes to have his or her own way, and it is a significant fact that nearly all the young ladies graduate as scientific students.

The work required in this course is not difficult, many students having no more than fifteen hours, the greater part of which is laboratory work. Of course there are others who take more hours and harder work, one student whom we have in mind has nineteen hours a week, twelve of which are devoted to art work and wood carving; we are glad to say that all do not have to work so hard.

These are the chief characteristics of the scientific course, and they are considered—by the students—to be very good indeed, for there are few people who do not like to have their own way, and many who do not enjoy hard work, and these are well suited to be "Scientific." Perhaps this is the reason that the number of scientific graduates is increasing each year.

The Brave Sophomores.

The room was peaceful and quiet,
   No signs of danger were near,
The class in Physics was listening,
   The words of wisdom to hear.

When, hark! a noise like thunder
   Breaks on their startled ears;
The frightened class-men shudder,
   Grow pale, overcome with their fears.

They look at the professor in terror,
   He, brave as a lion and bold,
Flings the closed door widely open
   And rushes out into the cold.

His example the class quickly followed,
   Over chairs, under tables they went—
Not until half way across the campus
   Was their energy entirely spent.

When the frightful sound had subsided
   ('Twas worse than the noise of a team),
The Sophs. slowly reëntered the classroom,
   And found it was only the steam.

And if one asks the Sophomores wise
   Why they madly rushed for the door,
They'll say 'twas merely for exercise,
   For Physics, you know, is a bore.

Lippitt Hall.

IN January, '97, the legislature granted to the college an appropriation of $45,000 for the erection of a new building. We had been sadly in need of such a building, being very much crowded through lack of enough recitation rooms. One of the rooms intended for students' living room had to be used for the mechanical drawing class, while physics was taught in an old wooden shanty at the back of the dormitory. Here also was kept the expensive physical apparatus. For a long time the State was unwilling to furnish the money, and it was not without a hard fight that it was finally granted. The great plea that was brought to bear upon the legislature was that there was no place in which to keep the government property belonging to the military department, and it was feared that the government would withdraw their military officer, and their yearly appropriation known as the Morrill Fund. All fear of such a dire calamity has, however, passed away, for we have our building, and much trouble has been taken to provide a place for the protection of the guns.

About half the basement and one-half the second floor is devoted to physics, the remaining half of the basement contains the electric lighting plant, consisting of an Armington & Sims high speed engine, and a 25 K. W. dynamo; and a 10 H. P. upright engine, and a 10 K. W. dynamo. This is also appropriated by the physical department. A whisper was at one time circulated that the whole building was to be used for physics, but somehow half of it was saved for other purposes, and we secured a room for the library, one for English, one for agriculture, and one for the use of the young women students. The cadets were fortunate in securing the top floor for a drill hall.

LIPPITT HALL.

About a month after the fall term opened the library was ready to receive the books then in our possession, so they were transferred by the students from the old wooden shanty, where they had been kept since the disastrous fire in the dormitory three years ago. Many more books have been added since, so that now we have a fairly well stocked library. Much attention has been paid to French and German, and a considerable part of our stock consists of books in those languages. They have never been read, and probably never will be, but they present quite an imposing appearance with their nice, new, unsoiled bindings. Our works of fiction are few, but good, but we think that the value and attractiveness of the library would be greatly enhanced by the addition of a great many more to our stock. The books are all catalogued on the card catalogue plan, and, to those who are initiated into the mysteries of its workings, it seems not to give so much trouble as one would expect; but to the uninitiated it is a confusion of confusions. However, it is the latest fad, and, as we must be up to date at any cost, we are perfectly satisfied with it; but when we want a book we walk around the shelves until we find it.

We use the drill hall as a gymnasium as well as we can with the small outfit that we have. The prospects of having a complete outfit are not very good at present, for we are told that to provide all that is necessary, other departments would have to be robbed. We have an outfit for playing basket ball, but the girls are the only ones who have an opportunity to play, for during the only hours which the boys have for playing the faculty or the Grange hold their meetings in the chapel underneath, and we are not allowed to play such a noisy game, because we disturb the meetings. We will not kick, however, but will accept with thankfulness the few crumbs which fall to our lot.

In Memoriam.

Where is now that gassy party that last year we used to know,
Gathered round the second table, Tennyson, Chaucer, all the go,
While at all the other tables everyone was hushed with awe.
How with bated breath we tried to catch some crumb from learn-
ing's store.

What a wondrous store of knowledge was unfolded to our ears.
Every time we heard them chinning we were almost moved to
tears.
And when some one spoke with feeling of the Canterbury tales,
From one place arose some laughter, others agonizing wails.

When in chapel one fine morning Mr. Drake a notice read,
One great member of that party felt like punching someone's head.
And other members, also, seemed struck with great surprise,
As though they'd never heard before of that club, great and wise.

Now, like the ancient nations of intellectual might,
This celebrated Chaucer club has vanished from our sight.
'Tis gone, but in our hearts and minds sad memories linger still;
With thankfulness that 'tis no more, our hearts at mealtimes fill.

General Calendar.

Sept. 21. College opens. Pearson gives Freshmen physical examination.
    23. Mr. Scott sets his memorial stone.
    28. Marsland sleeps while in charge of study room.
Oct. 1. Bicycle fiend appeared on lawn. Crandall appears in golf stockings.
    12. Taylor shows Congdon how to drop a cent down a lamp chimney.
    14. Fire in coop.
    15. Juniors give reception to Freshmen. Moffit makes a speech.
    17. Gump falls from grace.
    18. Alarm of fire on the escape. 'Rastus is rusticated for a month. By-gummy pin of engine busted.
    21. Dr. accuses electric wires of careless smoking.
Nov. 4. Jollie and Sisson withdraw from college.
    5. Students transfer books to new library. Ladd shows his authority by stopping dance on top floor.
    6. Company A beats Company B at football. Score, 10-0.
Dec. 3. Feast in No. 13 to celebrate Morrison's return. Reynolds and Munroe expelled from fourth floor.
    4. Rastus and H. Arnold go hunting porcupines.
    10. H. A——d threatened to punch G——t after drill, but did not do it.
    15. E. Payne borrows Miss Fison's umbrella to keep rain off Miss Thompson. Consequence—Miss Fison has to stay for an hour at the bot. lab.
    16. Sophomores frightened by the noise of the steam.
    17. Officers' ball. Horse runs away with Rufus.

Jan. 3. Winter term begins.
6. Payne returns. Said snow prevented him coming sooner, but forgot to say that it was because the sleighing was so good.
7. Pink waists and clam chowder for supper. Boys and girls very restless all night.
10. Willie called upon Miss G——d. Poultry class arrives. Much crowing in dormitory.
18. Dancing class formed.
28. Newton has a swim in bed. Explosion of hot water boiler.
31. Pat is lost. Search party goes out.

Feb. 3. Lecture by Mr. Fretwell. Some Juniors organize a sleigh ride, but it does not come off.
5. Sophomores have a sleigh ride, but find it rather damp.
6. Pink waist appears again. Archie walks home from church with Miss Spink.
10. Smith cuts supper.
11. Clarner swallows a pin.
12. Watson house celebrates Miss Putnam's ——th birthday.
14. Valentines for supper.
21. Freshmen sit up all night to catch the fellows who were going to duck Dingleberry, but found it was all a hoax.
22. Athletic Association give a dance. Newton varnishes his book case with glue.

Mar. 16. Brightman concocts some extraordinary advertisements.

Apr. 19. Miss Bosworth goes to Germany.
28. Alfred Bosworth comes out in golfs.
30. Miss Rockwell gives reception in drill hall. Pink waist for supper. Gump sick all night.

May 19. Capt. Wotherspoon leaves for the seat of war.
22. Junior Promenade.

Applied Quotations.

"Look you, I am the most concerned in my own interests."
—*Tucker.*

"I shall ne'er beware of mine own wit till I break my shin against it."—*Wightman.*

"Hail fellow, well met."—*Harley.*

"From the crown of his head to the sole of his foot he is all mirth."—*Cumming.*

"He is of a very melancholy disposition."—*Grant.*

"The mirror of all courtesy."—*H. Knowles.*

"Whatever sceptic could inquire for,
For every why she hath a wherefore."—*M. Flagg.*

"Ask me no questions and I'll tell you no lies."—*Morrison.*

"A progeny of learning."—*Chaucer.*

"Sharp's the word with her."—*A. Sherman.*

"Laugh and be fat."—*G. Soule.*

"Is she not passing fair."—*G. Wilson.*

"I am here; I shall remain here."—*S. Wright.*

"Her air, her manners, all who saw admired;
Courteous though coy, and gentle though retired."
—*Hurter.*

> "She is pretty to walk with
> And witty to talk with,
> And pleasant, too, to think on."
>
> —*S. Fison.*

> "Soft peace she brings wherever she arrives.
> She builds our quiet as she forms our lives;
> Lays the rough paths of peevish Nature even,
> And opens in each heart a little Heaven."—*Cargill.*

Nonsense.

Prof. S——. "Define 'Acoustics.'"

Y——w K——d. "Acoustics are long lines of wire with a kind of a box at each end to receive the sound."

Miss B——th. "Where do two lines intersect?"

Miss R——e. "Where they meet."

Capt. T——r. "Company: Open chambers—March."

Class in Latin. Mr. P——n translating. "And Cæsar dug a well sixteen feet high."

"Who hid the fire extinguisher, on the night of the fire, for fear that it would be burned?"

Prof. M ——d. "The explosion shook up my revolving bookcase, and the castors won't work now."

Mr. Cl——er. "Then all you need is a little castor oil to fix them."

Miss B——th. "You ar'nt Gray are you Grant."

Mr. L——d's definition of "cribbing." "A strategy by means of which some students evade a condition."

Miss P——m. "Are you all here?"

G——ll. "Yes, I am all here."

Miss P-——m. "I have seen the time when some members of the class did not seem to be all here."

Lieut. T——r. "What is extension of close order?"

G——ll. "Left forward! Fours left—No, I mean, fours right."

"Last year we thought Corpl. B——th was very much interested in Co. B; this year, as a Sergt., he is more interested in the Company of G(——d)."

R. E. G's definition of H_2O. "It is composed of O and H and hydraulic pressure."

Lieut. H——y. "Who is the leader of the squad?"
Priv. C. C——s. "The biggest man."

Some definitions from this year's Freshman class, in Physiology: "A skeleton is the bony frame of a dead man, put together like a live one." "Protoplasm is something which has no function except to get alive." "A cell is a round thing full of holes."

Evening of October 20, 1897. Dr. W——er (at back of building). "Fire, on fire escape." Investigations follow. Nothing but an old shirt found. Some mean person suggests that it might have been Grant's head that he saw.

Prof. B——. "What is curve tracing?"
C——gs. "Illustrated algebra."

Miss ——, who has recently been elected a member of the class, of little experience, conversing with the president of the same. "Shall I be allowed to come in at the class meetings now, Mr. President?"

The President. "I really don't know, but, if you like, I'll bring the matter before the class, and they may decide."

"S'asseoir" (pronounced "Sassey squaw"). Miss D——: "I didn't know, Miss S——, that the French had much knowledge of the Indians."

Sample page from a primer to be published by Gin & Co. Price 80 cents.

Ques. "Does Mr. O—— carry a fan to the dancing class?"

Ans. "Yes, Mr. O—— carries Miss G——n's fan to the dancing class."
Ques. "Why does Mr. O—— carry Miss G——n's fan?"
Ans. "Oh! He thinks it belongs to Miss P——."

Manuscripts for Sale.

"How to Harvest Ice." W. F. Owens.
"Wire Pulling." H. W. Arnold.
"How to Spoil a Storage Battery." M. A. Ladd.
"How to Civilize the Reubens." C. B. Morrison.
"Housekeeping in a Peanut Shell." The Misses James.
"Relaxation, or the Art of Rest." The Misses Stillman.
"Machine Shop Practice Made Easy." W. C. Phillips.
"Economical Methods of Stowing Away Provisions." G. R. Soule.
"How to Get Your Own Way." S. R. Thompson.

Narrow Escape.

Last summer two of our fellow students had a narrow escape from drowning in the Salt Pond. They started one afternoon for a sail in a small boat, when, at some distance from the shore, the boat capsized, filled, and went to the bottom; but the young men.

however, would not desert their ship—though they could not swim, like true American seamen, they stood by her to the last, and clung gallantly to the mast, which stood about two feet out of water. Their bravery might have cost them dear, but, by the time they were nearly exhausted, a fisherman came to their rescue and carried them ashore.

Great Minds Run in the Same Channel.

Scene in Room 21. Time 12:15. H—— K—— (in great excitement). "Say, P——, they have elected that d—— f—— of a H—— A—— on the board of editors."

Scene in the same room. Time 12:20. H—— A——. "Say, P——, they have elected that d—— f——, H—— K——, as a member of the board of editors."

A Poultry Problem.

I bought some fowls the other day;
One hundred dollars did I pay.
Each turkey did five dollars touch,
Each goose did bring but half as much;
While chickens, if it must be told,
For ten cents each were freely sold;
One hundred fowls in all had I,
Of each how many did I buy?

An Incident.

Sh——n, reading in Trig. class: "For the sake of brevity we shall hereafter make use of the following conventions."
Instructor. "What do you mean by that, Mr. Sh——n?"
Sh——n. "I don't just make out what it means."
Instructor. "Well, what is meant by conventions?"
Sh——n. "I don't really know. I have heard about Christian Endeavor Conventions before now. Is that it?"

Conundrums.

What is political economy?
Ans. Splitting your vote.

Why is a postman like a college professor?
Ans. Because he is a man of letters.

What is a cadet's best uniform?
Ans. Right dress.

What would you do if the dormitory caught fire?
Ans. Just look out the window and see the fire escape.

Why is M. R. Cross like the captain's dog, when tired?
Ans. Both come in short pants.

Why is Si's horse like Napoleon?
Ans. Because you can see the bony part.

Why does Pearson like to go into a barber's shop?
Ans. He likes to associate with the rest of the mugs.

What is Grant most of the time?
Ans. A-bed.

What happened to Newton's alarm clock after he brought it upstairs?
Ans. It ran down.

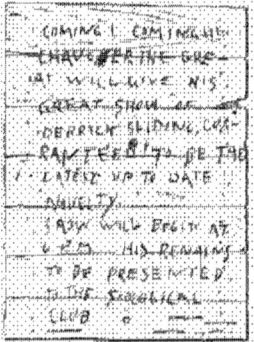

Facsimile of Chaucer's poster as it appeared on last announcement night.

STUDENTS AT DRILL.

Military Companies.

Commandant.
W. W. WOTHERSPOON, Capt. Twelfth Infantry, U. S. A.

Company A.
W. C. Clark	Captain.
W. F. Harley	First Lieutenant.

Sergeants.
S. W. Wright	1st Sergeant.
B. E. Kenyon	2d Sergeant.
H. A. Congdon	3d Sergeant.
G. Rose	4th Sergeant.
R. S. Doughty	5th Sergeant.

Corporals.
H. W. Arnold	1st Corporal.
W. C. Phillips	2d Corporal.
J. J. Fry	3d Corporal.
A. E. Munroe	4th Corporal.

Company B.
A. A. Tucker	Captain.
J. P. Case	2d Lieutenant.

Sergeants.
M. A. Ladd	1st Sergeant.
W. L. W. Clark	2d Sergeant.
A. W. Bosworth	3d Sergeant.
W. F. Owen	4th Sergeant.
H. Knowles	5th Sergeant.

Corporals.
C. Knowles	1st Corporal.
R. N. Soule	2d Corporal.
A. Pearson, Jr.	3d Corporal.
P. M. Greene	4th Corporal.

Lieutenant W. F. Harley	Battalion Adjutant.
H. W. Case	Bugler.

The Clubs.

Zoological Club.

Officers.

C. B. MORRISON, President.
A. PEARSON, Vice-President.
H. KNOWLES, Secretary.
E. PAYNE, Curator.

Members.

Miss Peckham,	Miss Putnam,
Miss McCrillis,	Miss Baldwin,
Dr. Field,	Dr. Wiggin,
W. L. W. Clarke,	J. R. Eldred,
R. S. Reynolds,	J. J. Fry,
P. K. Brady,	H. M. Brightman.
Miss Goddard,	Miss Hunter.

Research Club.

The Research Club meets weekly for the purpose of studying forms of literature, not included in the regular college course.

Officers.

H. W. ARNOLD, PRESIDENT.
M. E. RICE, SECRETARY AND TREASURER.

Members.

MISS PUTNAM,	MISS ROCKWELL,
A. W. BOSWORTH,	MISS HARVEY,
C. B. MORRISON,	H. KNOWLES,
JOHN WILBY,	E. PAYNE,
MISS GODDARD,	MISS GEORGE,

MISS PECKHAM.

Chemical Club.

Officers.

C. F. KENYON, President.
W. J. TAYLOR, Vice-President.
H. W. ARNOLD, Secretary.

Members.

Dr. Washburn,	Dr. Wheeler,
Dr. Field,	Prof. Scott,
Dr. Bucher,	Prof. Towar,
B. L. Hartwell,	C. B. Morrison,
H. Knowles,	Miss Baldwin,
Miss Bosworth.	

Eclectic Society.

Officers.

HARRIET F. TURNER, PRESIDENT.
WILLIAM L. W. CLARKE, VICE-PRESIDENT.
EDNA M. CARGILL, SECRETARY.

Executive Committee.

HARRIETE F. TURNER,   EDNA M. CARGILL,
WILLIAM L. W. CLARKE,   BERTHA D. TUCKER,
WILLIAM F. HARLEY.

Engineering Society.

Organized under the direction of Prof. Drake, for conference on special and current topics on mechanical engineering. Society meeting every two weeks.

Officers.

Prof. W. E. DRAKE, President.
C. S. CLARKE, Vice-President.
A. C. SCOTT, Secretary.

INFANTRY DRILL.

The Associations.

College Alumni Association.

HOWLAND BURDICK,
PRESIDENT.

GEORGE A. RODMAN,
SECRETARY.

CHARLES L. SARGENT,
TREASURER.

Y. M. C. A.

HENRY M. BRIGHTMAN,
PRESIDENT.

EDGAR R. PIPER,
VICE-PRESIDENT.

ALFRED W. BOSWORTH,
CORRESPONDING AND RECORDING SECRETARY.

H. D. SMITH,
TREASURER.

Young Women's Christian Union.

MILDRED HARVEY,
PRESIDENT.

BERTHA BENTLEY,
VICE-PRESIDENT.

ELIZABETH PARKHURST,
SECRETARY.

S. LILA JAMES,
TREASURER.

Athletics.

ATHLETICS, as an established line of student effort, were introduced in our college, when, in 1892, a few spirited individuals organized themselves into an athletic association, which in the succeeding years has gradually been placed on a more secure basis by the student body. Many difficulties have been faced, but our association has proven itself equal to the emergencies, and as a result of toilsome labors has become one of the most prominent organizations in State College athletics.

It is greatly to our credit that we have developed teams that have been able to cope with others far superior in training, and have held them down to small scores, and in a number of cases have turned the game against them.

In base-ball we feel that our greatest progress has been made, and, with the combined effort of faculty and students, hope, in succeeding years, to place teams on the diamond that R. I. C. may well be proud to claim.

This year has been one of our most successful years, and the outlook for the future is encouraging.

Athletic Association.

1897-98.

MORTON R. CROSS,
PRESIDENT.

HAROLD W. CASE,
VICE-PRESIDENT.

WILLIAM C. CLARK,
SECRETARY.

PROF. J. D. TOWAR.
TREASURER.

Foot-Ball.

W. F. OWEN, Manager.

'Varsity Eleven.

R. S. Doughty (Capt.), *l. h.*, H. P. Wilson, *l. t.*,
W. F. Owen, *r. h.*, R. E. Grinnell, *l. g.*,
W. C. P. Merrill, *f. b.*, G. C. Soule, *c.*,
M. R. Cross, *q. b.*, W. F. Harley, *r. g.*,
A. A. Denico, *l. e.*, J. R. Emmett, *r. t.*,
W. G. Clark, *r. e.*

Substitutes.

J. J. Fry, H. W. Case,
D. N. Newton, Jr., W. S. Bacheller.

Games Played.

Oct. 16. R. I. C. *vs.* New London, at New London. 0–6.
Oct. 23. R. I. C. *vs.* Storrs Agr. College, at New London. 8–22.
Nov. 13. R. I. C. *vs.* Pawtucket High School. 22–0.

Base-Ball.

H. W. ARNOLD, MANAGER.

Varsity Nine.

W. F. OWEN, (Capt.), c.,   T. C. RILEY, 3 b.,
P. BRADY, p.,   R. S. REYNOLDS, s. s.,
H. P. WILSON, 1 b.,   A. A. TUCKER, l. f.,
E. T. ARNOLD, 2 b.,   W. C. P. MERRILL, c. f.,
                C. S. BURGESS, r. f.

Substitutes.

C. C. CROSS.   J. J. FRY.
                M. R. CROSS.

Games Played.

Apr. 9.   R.I.C. vs. Bulkely School, at Kingston.   3-8.
Apr. 13. R.I.C. vs. Westerly High School, at Kingston.   19-4.
Apr. 16. R.I.C. vs. East Greenwich, at East Greenwich.   11-13.
Apr. 23. R.I.C. vs. Westerly Athletic, at Kingston.   22-3.
Apr. 27. R.I.C. vs. Bulkely School, at New London. 13-11 (10 ins.).
May 4.   R.I.C. vs. Storrs Agr. College, at Storrs.   24-8 (6 ins.).
May 7.   R.I.C. vs. Rogers High School, at Kingston.   7-5.
May 10.   R.I.C. vs. Paw. High School, at Kingston.   14-7 (6 ins.).

Scheduled Games.

May 14.   R.I.C. vs. Brown 1900, Kingston.
May 21.   R.I.C. vs. Friends School, Providence.
May 28.   R.I.C. vs. East Greenwich, Kingston.
June 4.   R.I.C. vs. Rogers High School, Newport.

An Improved Opportunity.

IT was a beautiful spring day in the country. The April wind was blowing gently over the hills and through the valleys. It was the glad awakening from the long, dismal, dreary winter. The leaves had not appeared, but the tiny buds were ready to burst forth when the rains and sunshine had coaxed them a little more. Everything was fresh and clear. Could one but be thankful for living? But there is another side. Human nature is the same, no matter what the weather. When the sun shines the very brightest, there are aching hearts and passionate tempers. They do not wait for a cloudy day to manifest themselves.

A girl came away from the house at the foot of the hill, and walked slowly up the road to her favorite seat—a large, flat stone, at the bottom of the stone wall which separated the roadway from the fields on the hillside beneath her. Her mood was not a pleasant one. She always came here when there was anything troubling her. The pines above her usually murmured some sweet, soothing story in their own sad language, and she was comforted. It seemed as though she understood them. She gazed about her, but did not appreciate the beauty of her surroundings. It was plain that she was very much agitated, and she held, in her hand, a letter, which had been opened. Away in the west Mt. Wachuset loomed up, big and round. The tiny house at the top was plainly visible. Further away, in New Hampshire, the mountains were enveloped in a charming purple haze. Trees, trees, hills and blue sky, were all that could be seen.

"The idea of their writing me such a letter! Why do they ask me to care for these children? They know perfectly well that I have more now than I can do. It does not seem as though I could give up everything. Was it wrong for me to make such rigid plans, with no thought of their ever being broken?"

Alice Hadly was a pretty, interesting girl of eighteen. When about to enter college she was called home to live with her stepmother on the farm. It was a bitter disappointment to her, but she tried not to drift backward. By studying she kept her mind alert and open. But another burden had been added. They were going to send the motherless grandchildren of her step-mother here for her to care for. She did rebel against it—out here alone—but when she returned to the house she was quite submissive. The sunshine and fresh air certainly had good effect upon her bitter mood.

The children were received some days later. Alice put forth every effort to reconcile herself to her fate, and to be kind and patient. But it was very hard work. Her life was a daily torture. No one in the house was in sympathy with her aims and desires. The atmosphere was cold and uncongenial. "How can I study when there is always someone at my elbow to say cheeringly: 'What good'll them things ever do yer?' It is worse than horrible!"

This girl was intellectual and imaginative. Of course the people around her did not understand. They had never been accustomed to looking at life from any other than the bread-and-butter standpoint. Her mind must have an outlet in some manner. There was no one to converse with. No cultured mind with which she could commune, so she wrote. Her desk was filled with stories. She sent one to a magazine, simply for the sake of knowing that she had tried. She expected it to be rejected, but hoped they would not say "Returned with thanks." But it was not so. The story was accepted, and accompanied by a very kind note from the editor. It was rare, and her first story too. But it meant so much to her. It encouraged her to try again. Up to this time she had been quite hopeless. One man had told her to read the lives of eminent men and women, to see that they had reached no great height until they had suffered. Her reply was defiant and pointed: "I have, and noticed that in almost every instance they had environment and hereditary culture in their favor. How do you expect me to concentrate my mind upon 'higher things' in this social atmosphere of mental depravity?"

She kept on, however, with her writing. Many of her stories gained a market. She lived a new life now. The home people were proud of her work. Proud, now! They had done all in their power to retard and discourage her, but, now that she had accomplished an end by her unaided efforts, they congratulated themselves that *they* had done so much.

The fuller, deeper seriousness of life now appealed to her. She knew that, unless she put out a supreme effort, her life would advance no further. She studied and worked, all for a definite object. The incongruities of the home life were easier to bear with this greater light in the distance.

The life was suddenly changed in the sleepy farm home. Her grandmother's children were sent to their father's sister. Alice was alone. She was free. A feeling of remorse came over her as she thought how often she had dared to wish herself free. "My hateful, selfish disposition! How unhappy I must have made them all."

When affairs were settled, Alice found herself penniless, with the exception of the money received from her stories. She was obliged to go to work, but there was little she was fitted for. A wealthy aunt wished to keep her and introduce her into society, but Alice's independent spirit revolted at the idea. For two years she worked in an office, among dry, prosy books. Her evenings and holidays were spent in study and writing. Her stories grew in favor, and she was nearing her goal.

It was a happy day when she left the office for the last time. Her examinations, for entrance to one of our most noted female colleges, were passed successfully. Her way was clear, at last.

.   .   .   .

There is a school and home in one of our large cities, where young men and women are educated for nearly every department in life. Great care is exercised in accepting students. Many who are not poor, yet are not rich enough to obtain a liberal education, are helped here.

Respectable poverty is the hardest to bear.

At the head of this grand work is a woman under thirty-five years of age. It is the girl, who, years ago, made such a desperate struggle for her advancement. Her money is the financial basis of the school; her talent and intellect the life of many restricted youths.

Did not her first story open a wide field? Who says we have no opportunities? N. H. P.

Advertisements.

List of Advertisers.

Armstrong & Sons, Wakefield,	14
Arnold & Maine, Providence,	5
Babcock, Geo. E., Westerly,	20
Babcock, E. M., Wakefield,	16
Ballou, F. E., Providence,	8
Barber, H. R., Wakefield,	9
Barbour & Stedman, Wakefield,	22
Bell, L. F., Wakefield,	22
Blanding & Blanding, Providence,	14
Bradley, A. E., Wakefield,	19
Brightman, J. F., Westerly,	20
Brown, B. F. & Son, Kingston,	15
Browne, C. L., Wakefield,	9
Carpenter, James, Peace Dale,	22
Colt, J. B. & Co., New York,	6
Coombs, H. M. & Co., Providence,	14
Covelle, H. J., Wakefield,	11
Crescent Cycle Co., Wakefield,	11
Dixon, L. & Co., Peace Dale,	16
Eimer & Amend, New York,	5
Eldred Bros., Wakefield,	15
Fagan, James, Rocky Brook,	22
Fagan, John, Peace Dale,	22
Fison, H. W., Peace Dale,	16
Flint & Co., Providence,	18
Freeman, E. L. & Sons, Central Falls,	1
Gillies' Sons, Wakefield,	4
Gould, W. G., Peace Dale,	16
Greenman, A. A., Kingston,	10

Griffin, W. H. & Co., Narragansett Pier, .	22
Helme, B. E., Kingston, .	7
Hodge, E. S., Peace Dale, .	17
Holt, S. N., Wakefield, .	12
Heald & Erickson, Providence, .	17
Horton Bros., Providence,	21
Hunt, J. J., Peace Dale,	16
Kenyon, Wakefield, .	11
Leslie, M., Wakefield, .	15
Libby, A., Peace Dale, .	13
Mumford, Miss, Wakefield, .	19
Mumford, J. A., Wakefield,	12
Olney, F. C., Wakefield,	22
Palmer, B. W., Wakefield, .	13
Potter, W. A. & Co., Providence,	12
Rathbun, W. S., Wakefield,	9
Reilly, L., Wakefield, .	22
Reuter, S. J., Westerly, .	4
Robinson, Wakefield, .	6
R. I. College, .	2
R. I. News Co., Providence,	7
Shannon, D. W., Wakefield,	4
Sheldon, G. H., Wakefield,	7
Sheldon, J. L., Wakefield,	10
Stiles, Westerly, .	20
Tucker, E. P. & S. L., West Kingston,	19
Tefft, J. A., Peace Dale,	19
Walker, J. S., Wakefield,	9
Wilcox, J. A., Wakefield,	22
Wilcox, H., Wakefield, .	22
Woods, Paul, Wakefield,	4
Wright, S. G., Wakefield,	10

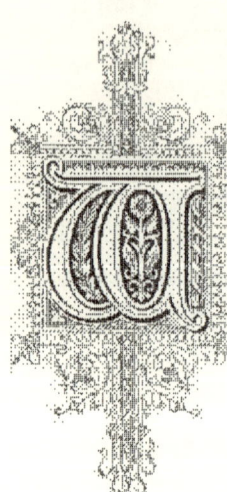HEN You need a Doctor

You don't hunt for a Quack — and

When You Want a Lawyer

You don't look for a Shyster.

You Want the Best and the Surest.
Act on the same line when you want a Printer.

IT PAYS.   That's why we say— without egotism—   COME TO US.

E. L. Freeman & Sons,

PRINTERS AND STATIONERS.

Providence Office: Pawtucket Office:
3 WESTMINSTER STREET.   239 MAIN STREET.

WORKS AT CENTRAL FALLS, R. I.

We are General Printers, and have exceptional facilities for printing Catalogues, Reports, Tax Books, Genealogies, Histories, and similar work, requiring a large plant and brains. This book is a fair sample. Send for estimates on anything......

R. I. College of Agriculture and Mechanic Arts.

TECHNICAL INSTRUCTION in agriculture, the mechanic arts, and the sciences. The four-year courses lead to the degree of Bachelor of Science, and after September, 1897, will be six in number: the course in agriculture, in mechanics, in chemistry, in physics and mathematics, in biology, and the general course. Special courses and a short course in agriculture and mechanics. The courses offered to men are also open to women.

INSTRUCTION IS GIVEN IN

Chemistry.—Inorganic, organic, agricultural, physiological and sanitary, and the chemistry of the dyeing of textile fabrics. Laboratory practice, both qualitative and quantitative.

Physics.—Especial attention being given to electricity, and to photography and projection.

Physiography.—With laboratory work and excursions.

Agricultural Geology.—With especial relation to the formation of soils.

Botany.—The later part of the course takes up the study of seed-plants of economic importance.

Comparative Anatomy and Physiology.—Veterinary science, physiological psychology, civil government, and political economy.

Zoology and Animal Biology.

Agriculture.—Theoretical and practical. Drainage, farm crops, stock-breeding, feeding of animals, fertilizers, dairying, apiary work.

Horticulture.—Olericulture, floriculture, pomology, vegetable pathology, horticultural literature, landscape gardening.

Languages and History.—English, comprising composition, rhetoric and literature; GERMAN—grammar, dictation, conversation, translation, reading; FRENCH; LATIN; expression, including sight reading, extemporaneous speaking, recitations, and original orations; history, American, English, and general.

Mathematics.— Including civil engineering and astronomy.

Mechanical Engineering.— Strength of materials, mechanism, mechanics of engineering, steam engineering, metallurgy, mechanical drawing, wood-working, forging, iron work, pattern making, machine construction.

Freehand Drawing and Modelling.

Military Drill and Tactics.— Required of all male students. Infantry, artillery and signal drill, lectures on military science.

FACILITIES FOR INSTRUCTION

Include an excellent library, well equipped laboratories for chemistry, botany, mechanics and biology, the latter having a large collection of Rhode Island birds; and a farm embracing a large variety of soils for the departments of agriculture and horticulture. The location is especially advantageous for work in zoology.

ADMISSION TO ADVANCED STANDING is granted to candidates prepared for the work of any of the higher classes.

EXPENSES. Per year:— Room rent, $6; board, $108; fuel, $12; light, $3 to $9; books, $15 to $30; washing, $10 to $20; reading-room tax, $.75; general expense, $1.50; laboratory fees, $6 to $30. Uniform, $15. Total for year,— minimum, $170; maximum, $250. Students of ability have opportunity to earn enough to pay a portion of their expenses.

EXPENSE FOR WOMEN. Board, including room rent, $3 per week; fuel and lights supplied at cost. Rooms furnished. Other expenses as above.

REQUIREMENTS FOR ADMISSION, 1897. Advanced arithmetic; geography; English grammar; United States History. No students admitted under fifteen years of age.

REQUIREMENTS FOR 1898. Arithmetic, algebra, plane geometry, English grammar, advanced English; United States history; geography, physiology; one year of German, French, or Latin.

A PREPARATORY DEPARTMENT will be opened in 1898.

Further details concerning the entrance requirements, with other information will be found in the catalogue, to be had on application to the President.

JOHN H. WASHBURN,

KINGSTON, R. I.

Fine Roses and Carnations

At Wholesale and Retail our Specialty. We Guarantee the Superiority of our Floral Work for Parties, Weddings, or Funerals.

S. J. REUTER, FLORIST

WESTERLY, R. I.

ORDERS BY MAIL, TELEGRAPH, OR TELEPHONE, RECEIVE PROMPT ATTENTION.

.....THE Printing WE DO, IS

Well Done, Promptly Done,
AND
Reasonably Done.

D. GILLIES' SONS,

TIMES PRINTING OFFICE.   WAKEFIELD, R. I.

D. W. SHANNON,

WAKEFIELD, R. I.

PAUL WOODS,

Builder,

AND DEALER IN

Fine Carriages.

REPAIRING OF ALL KINDS A SPECIALTY.

WAKEFIELD, R. I.

Jena Normal Glass, The Glass of the Future.

ESTABLISHED 1851.

EIMER & AMEND,

Manufacturers and Importers of

Chemicals and Chemical Apparatus.

Kahlbaum's Famous Chemicals and Reagents.
Finest Bohemian and German Glassware.
Royal Berlin and Meissen Porcelain.
Purest Hammered Platinum.
Finest Balances and Weights.
Zeiss Microscopes.
And Bacteriological Apparatus.
Chemically Pure Acids.
And Assay Goods.
Everything Necessary for the Laboratory.

205, 207, 209 & 211

THIRD AVENUE,

Corner of 18th Street,

NEW YORK.

THE MAMMOTH
New England Grocery & Tea House,

93 to 101 WEYBOSSET STREET,

PROVIDENCE, R. I.

BRANCHES AT PAWTUCKET AND WORCESTER.

The Stores are the largest of their kind in each of the cities. They are Headquarters of all classes of consumers from the smallest to the largest, both in the cities and surrounding country. Twenty-six years of uninterrupted, healthy business have given them an acquaintance in almost every State in the Union, and they are not surprised to receive orders from East, West, North or South.

PRICE LISTS, COMPLETE TO DATE, MAILED FREE TO ANY ADDRESS.

B. F. ARNOLD.   H. E. MAINE.

SEARCH LIGHTS CUBAN WAR
FOR PLEASURE BOATS. ILLUSTRATED.

Lantern Slides in Great Variety.

ACETYLENE GAS GENERATORS FOR ALL PURPOSES, GIVING THE MOST PERFECT ARTIFICIAL LIGHT KNOWN. SAFE AND ECONOMICAL.

Magic Lanterns AND *Stereopticons,*

THE LARGEST AND BEST STOCK IN AMERICA.

♦ ♦ ♦ ♦ ♦ ♦ ♦

We have them all.   Write for information and mention "The Grist."

J. B. COLT & CO.,

Manufacturers of
"Everything for the Lanternist."   *3 to 7 West 29th Street,*

NEW YORK.

ROBINSON'S

ESTABLISHED 1821.   .....WAKEFIELD, R. I.

Grocers.

Imported and Domestic Fancy Groceries, Table Delicacies.

OUR SPECIALTY:

TEA, COFFEE, FANCY CRACKERS,

Cigars and Tobacco.   Pillsbury Flour.   Ferris Hams and Bacon.

The Rhode Island News Company,

139 & 141 Westminster Street, Providence, R. I.

Books: { Agricultural, Miscellaneous, Educational, Juvenile. **Stationery:** { Everything Needed For School and Office.

Sporting Goods: { Bicycles and Bicycle Sundries. Base Ball Goods. Tennis Goods. Fishing Tackle. **Periodicals:** { By Single Number. Subscriptions at Lowest Rates.

LARGEST STOCK.   LOWEST PRICES.

THE RHODE ISLAND NEWS COMPANY,

139 & 141 Westminster Street, Providence, R. I.

B. E. HELME,

Kingston, R. I.

DRY ✦ GOODS

—AND—

GROCERIES.

FINE CONFECTIONERY.

Lowney's Chocolates.

GEO. H. SHELDON,

Agent for the Spalding Bicycles. *News Dealer and Stationer.*

ALSO DEALER IN

ALL KINDS OF SPORTING GOODS

Base Ball, Foot Ball, Golf, Tennis, and Bicycle Supplies.

188 Main St., Wakefield, R. I.

Cosy Corner in the
F. E. Ballou Shoe Emporium,
Weybosset and Eddy Streets,   .   .   .   Providence, R. I.

Prof. C. L. Browne,

INIMITABLE
Hair Cutter.

My line of Hair Cutting consists of the following styles: The Business Cut, Young American, Crescent, and the Regulation Pompadour. I also make a Specialty of the English Oxford A-La-Mode.

Try Browne's Facial Cream for Rough and Chapped Face or Hands. It imparts a Soft and Velvety Texture to the Skin. It is also good for Sunburn and Pimples.

Main Street, Wakefield, R. I.
OPPOSITE BAPTIST CHURCH.

"Keep Your Shirt On"

But, if you take it off, send it to the

Narragansett Laundry.

Where it will be promptly done up in a satisfactory manner.

All Kinds of Laundry Work Solicited.

JOHN S. WALKER, Prop.

WAKEFIELD, R. I.

Henry R. Barber,

DEALER IN
Eastern, Western and Southern Rough and Dressed

LUMBER,

WINDOWS, DOORS, BLINDS AND MOULDINGS.

Brick, Lime, Cement, Hair and Drain Pipe.

Builders' Hardware a Specialty.

WAKEFIELD AND WICKFORD, R. I.

DR. W. S. RATHBUN,

Veterinary Surgeon

AND

DENTIST.

CASTRATION, DENTISTRY, SICK AND LAME HORSES TREATED BY THE LATEST SCIENTIFIC METHODS.

Office: *Wright Drug Store,*
Residence, - - Orchard Avenue,

WAKEFIELD, R. I.

JOHN L. SHELDON,

Successor to G. W. SHELDON CO.

FURNI-TURE,
And General House Furnishings.

STOVES, FURNACES, RANGES,

GLASS, TIN AND WOODEN WARE.

Plumbing and Tinsmithing In All Its Branches.

WAKEFIELD, R. I.

If you want to buy your

DRUGS AND MEDICINES

AT CITY PRICES,

YOU WILL CALL ON

S. G. WRIGHT, *Wakefield, R. I.*

→✶ A. A. GREENMAN, ✶←

DEALER IN

GROCERIES, DRY GOODS,

ETC., ETC.

KINGSTON, R. I.

Why do Riders buy more CRESCENTS than any other make of Wheel?
Because they are the Most Popular Wheel made.

83,000 MADE AND SOLD IN 1897.

We have the Most Complete Line of Wheels in South Kingstown.

CLIPPER, WHITE, RAMBLER, TRIBUNE, LOVELL DIAMOND, IDEAL, AND .....OWEN BICYCLES.....

Bicycles & Tandems for Rent by the Day, Week, or Season.

We make a Specialty of CAMERAS and SUPPLIES.   A Fresh Stock Constantly on hand.
POCO and PREMO CAMERAS.

A well equipped repair department in connection with our salesroom.
Our work is guaranteed satisfactory.   Open all the year round.

Crescent Cycle Co., Opposite Wakefield Depot, **WAKEFIELD, R. I.**

Kenyon's AT WAKEFIELD,

IS THE PLACE TO BUY YOUR
DRY ✦ GOODS.

H. J. COVELLE,

MAKES A SPECIALTY OF FITTING GLASSES, AND OCULISTS' PRESCRIPTION WORK.

Jeweler and Optician.

Repairing of All Kinds.   **WAKEFIELD, R. I.**

Compliments of ————

Walter A. Potter
& Co.

SEEDSMEN AND DEALERS IN AGRICULTURAL IMPLEMENTS.

6 Exchange Place, - Providence, R. I.

J. A. MUMFORD,

34, 36 & 38 MAIN STREET,
WAKEFIELD, R. I.

HACK,
BOARDING,
SALE AND
LIVERY
STABLE.

The Largest Stable in Wakefield, where can be found a Large Line of Single and Double Teams, Hacks, Wagonettes, Surreys, Single and Double Carriages, Party Wagons, Etc.

Funerals, Weddings, Picnic Parties accommodated at Short Notice. Open day and Night.

TELEPHONE No. 7102-4.

KEEP YOUR EYE ON THE
→ *CRIMSON RIMS.*

We are Headquarters
for the Famous

Syracuse Bicycle, Price $50.

Other Grades $25 Up.

ALSO, FIRST-CLASS REPAIRING.

S. N. HOLT,
COLUMBIA CORNER, WAKEFIELD.

B. W. PALMER,

DEALER IN

MEN'S, BOYS' AND CHILDREN'S

HATS, CAPS, GENTS' FURNISHINGS, BICYCLE CLOTHING,

Men's and Boys' Boots and Shoes.

MAIN STREET, - WAKEFIELD, R. I.

A. LIBBY,

Horse Shoeing

— AND —

General Jobbing.

High Street, ✠ Peace Dale, R. I.

Carriages. *Carriages.*

VISIT THE FACTORY OF
C. H. ARMSTRONG & SONS,
WAKEFIELD, R. I.

Besides being the Sole Manufacturers of the Improved Armstrong Buckboard, we are also Builders of all styles of Carriages, a fine assortment of which can always be seen at our Wakefield Repository. We are now making a specialty of

DELIVERY AND DEPOT WAGONS, TRAPS OF ALL KINDS.

Suitable for any business. For the best made carriage in the world, and lowest price, call on

C. H. ARMSTRONG & SONS.

BLANDING & BLANDING,
Wholesale and Retail Druggists.

PHYSICIAN'S PRESCRIPTIONS A SPECIALTY.

54 and 58 WEYBOSSET STREET, - **PROVIDENCE, R. I.**

H. M. Coombs.   ESTABLISHED 1860.   N. J. SMITH.

H. M. COOMBS & CO.,
Blank Book Makers, Paper Rulers and Book Binders.

BINDERS TO THE STATE.

15 CUSTOM HOUSE STREET,   **PROVIDENCE, R. I.**

ELDRED BROS.,

DEALERS IN

High=Grade Groceries,  AND FRESH MEATS.

FRUITS, VEGETABLES, ETC.

95 Main Street, - - Wakefield, R. I.

Miss Leslie,

Fashionable

 Dress Making.

Prices Reasonable.

Bank Building, Wakefield, R. I.

B. F. Brown & Son,

DEALERS IN

Beef, Pork, Mutton,

and

Poultry.

KINGSTON, R. I.

FURNITURE!

.....A FULL LINE OF

Chamber Sets, Brass Trimmed Enameled Beds, with Woven Wire Springs.

Dining Tables, Chairs, Rockers, Chiffonieres, Couches, Lounges.

Carpets, Japanese and China Mattings.

WALL PAPERS WITH BORDERS TO MATCH.

Special Attention Given to Window Shade Work.

J. J. HUNT, ✷✷ PEACE DALE, R. I.

W. G. Gould, PEACE DALE, R. I.

DEALER IN

Dry and Fancy Goods,

GROCERIES,

Boots, Shoes and Rubbers,

AND A COMPLETE LINE OF THE PEACE DALE MFG. CO.'S GOODS.

Babcock Bazaar.

DRY GOODS,

Fancy Crockery & Tinware.

E. M. BABCOCK,

WAKEFIELD, R. I.

Miss L. Dixon & Co.

Millinery.

PEACE DALE, R. I.

New Mail Bicycle   Hanover Bicycle
Price, $65.00.   Price, $45.00.

STRICTLY HIGH GRADE.

HERBERT W. FISON, Agent,

PEACE DALE, R. I.

Liberal Discount for Cash.

E. S. HODGE,
PEACE DALE, R. I.
Plumbing, Steam & Gas Fitting.

SPECIAL ATTENTION GIVEN TO
STEAM, HOT WATER AND HOT AIR
HEATING.

AGENT FOR THE FAMOUS GLENWOOD RANGES.

CLASS.....
PHOTOGRAPHER
TO
Rhode Island College of Agriculture and Mechanic Arts, '98.
Warren High School, '98.
Providence High School, '98.

MODERN TASTE IN PHOTOGRAPHY.

THE distribution of High-Grade Workmanship, characterized by that subtle treatment in pose and technique is the standard by which our reputation and very large patronage have been gained. . . . .

SPECIAL RATES FOR COLLEGE AND SCHOOL WORK.

In Crayon and Pastel Work, our success has been remarksble.

One Moment Please. **FLINT CO.**

WILL FURNISH YOUR NEED IN THE LINE OF *Furniture.*

CARPETS, CLOTHING, BICYCLES, ETC.

MOST LIBERAL CREDIT SYSTEM ON EARTH. REMEMBER, NO TROUBLE TO SHOW GOODS.

Weybosset & Eddy Sts.

Established 1862.

Notice !

SHOWER BATHS May be had Free at Any Time between 6:30 and 7:30 P. M., on the Front Slope of Davis Hall, and, after 10:30 P. M., Anywhere Inside the Hall.

Applications Should Be Handed to Ђ. R- -s Before Supper.

THIS LIE LACKS STRAWBERRIES.

MISS ANNIE E. BRADLEY,

Millinery,

BANK BLOCK, WAKEFIELD.   BRICK BLOCK, WICKFORD.

James A. Tefft,
..Florist and Market Gardener..
Peace Dale, R. I.

Carnations and Violets in their Season.   Decorating Plants for Rental and Sale.

HOUSE CLOSED ON SATURDAY.

E. P. & S. L. Tucker,
WEST KINGSTON, R. I.
General Store,
DEALERS IN
Dry Goods, Boots and Shoes,

Gents' Furnishing Goods, Flour, Grain and Groceries, and General Farm Supplies. Also Anthracite Coal at Wholesale and Retail. Agent for the Swift-Lowell Fertilizer Company.

Special Attention Given to Orders for Goods Not Kept in Stock.

MRS. MUMFORD,
Fashionable Milliner,

MAIN STREET,
WAKEFIELD, R. I.

YOUR DUTY TO YOUR FRIENDS, IS THAT YOU HAVE A GOOD AND RECENT PICTURE OF YOURSELF.

I Spare No Pains To obtain the most pleasing results, Giving you the Light and Position Best Adapted to your Features. **Stiles, The Photographer.**
(BROWN BUILDING.)

HIGH STREET, WESTERLY, R. I.

WOMEN Are the final judges of the becomingness of Men's Clothes. Every man's mother, sister, or wife, is sure to have something to say about his clothes. In ninety cases out of a hundred, the pleasure or displeasure he will take in his new suit or overcoat will be based upon the opinions they express in them. ..... Any garment in our store, which, after purchase, does not please either yourself or friends, we will take back and refund the purchase money without argument or protest........ ;~ As often as possible the people shall buy here for less than anywhere else.

GEO. H. BABCOCK, Westerly, R. I.

16, 18 & 20 Main Street.

Tiger Bicycles. "BEST IN THE WORLD."

MADE BY THE
STODDARD MFG. CO.,
Of Dayton, Ohio.

Three Paramount Issues: Lightness, Strength, and Simplicity of Adjusting Bearings.

These three are contained in these wheels. Our line consists of the following:

TIGER, $50, FOUR SIZES.   TIGRESS, $50, THREE SIZES.
TIGER SPECIAL, $75, THREE SIZES.   TIGRESS SPECIAL, $75, THREE SIZES.
BOYS' AND GIRLS' $35 AND $40, FOUR SIZES.
LADIES' AND GENTS' CYGNETS IN FIVE SIZES, $75.   SEND FOR CATALOGUE.

JOS. F. BRIGHTMAN, - AGENT,
107 Main Street,   Westerly, R. I.

HORTON BROS.

Opposite Shepard & Co.   *256 Westminster Street,*

PROVIDENCE, R. I.

High Grade of Work at Reasonable Prices.

NEW STUDIO,   *With Unsurpassed Facilities.*

Elevator.

L. F. BELL,

Contractor & Builder,

Wakefield, R. I.

FREDERICK C. OLNEY,

Attorney and Counsellor at Law.

WAKEFIELD, R. I.

HORACE WILCOX, M. D.,

Physician and Surgeon,

WAKEFIELD, R. I.

Main Street, - - Near Prospect Avenue.

Telephone 7118-4.

Office Hours: 8 to 9 A. M., 1 to 3, and 7 to 9 P. M.

John Fagan,

DEALERS IN

FINE GROCERIES,

Boots, Shoes & Rubbers.

Peace Dale, R. I.

Miss L. Reilly,

MILLINER.

Main St., Wakefield, R. I.

James Carpenter,

PIANO TUNER.

Teacher of Violin, Cornet, etc.

Maker and Repairer of all Musical Instruments.

Peace Dale, R. I.

JAMES FAGAN,

→ VARIETY STORE. ←

CIGARS, TOBACCO, AND CONFECTIONERY,

ROCKY BROOK, R. I.

J. A. WILCOX, M. D.,

※ ※ ※

Telephone 7208-4.

Wakefield, R. I.

J. C. Barbour.   O. E. Stedman.

♥ ♥

Dentistry,

♥ ♥

Robinson Street, Wakefield.

WM. H. GRIFFITH & CO.,

PLUMBERS,

97 CAMBRIDGE ST., - - BOSTON.

Branch, Narragansett Pier, R. I.

www.ingramcontent.com/pod-product-compliance
Lightning Source LLC
Chambersburg PA
CBHW031402160426
43196CB00007B/868